PALMS
IN COLOUR

PALMS
IN COLOUR

Australian
Natives
& Exotics

David L. Jones

REED

Acknowledgements

I thank Barbara Jones for processing the manuscript
and Dennis Hundscheidt, Jim Willis, Clyde Dunlop,
Bruce Gray and Chris Goudey for allowing me to use
their photographs as credited.

First published 1985
Reprinted in 1989, 1991

REED BOOKS PTY LTD
3/470 Sydney Rd. Balgowlah NSW 2093

© David Jones 1985

National Library of Australia
Cataloguing-in-Publication Data

Jones, David L. (David Lloyd), 1944-
    Palms in color.
    ISBN 0 7301 0110 X.
    1. Palms – Australia. 2. House plants. I. Title.
635.9'345'0994

Typeset by Deblaere Typesetting Pty Ltd.
Printed In Singapore Through
Imago Productions (FE) Pte. Ltd.

CONTENTS

INTRODUCTION

Palms are becoming a very popular group of plants with gardeners, especially in tropical regions where conditions are favourable for the growth of a wide range of species. The trend is also noticeable in temperate climes, although here the number of species which can be grown is much less. A significant group of palms is also making an impact in the range of plants successfully used for indoor decoration. Palms are easily grown and a good range is commonly available from specialist nurseries.

Palms are a very obvious group of plants easily recognisable because of their distinctive growth habit but some people confuse them with plants having a similar appearance (Cordylines, Cycads, Bananas, etc.). Botanically speaking, palms are woody members of the major group of plants belonging to the monocotyledons (this means that all have a single seed leaf) and are placed in the plant family Arecaceae.

There are about 3000 species of palms and these belong in about 220 genera. They are widely distributed in the well-watered zones of the world but are absent or rare in very dry or very cold regions. Palms are most common in tropical vegetation and are noticeable among shrubs and trees because of their distinctive silhouettes. A few species may grow in extensive colonies, others are found as solitary individuals

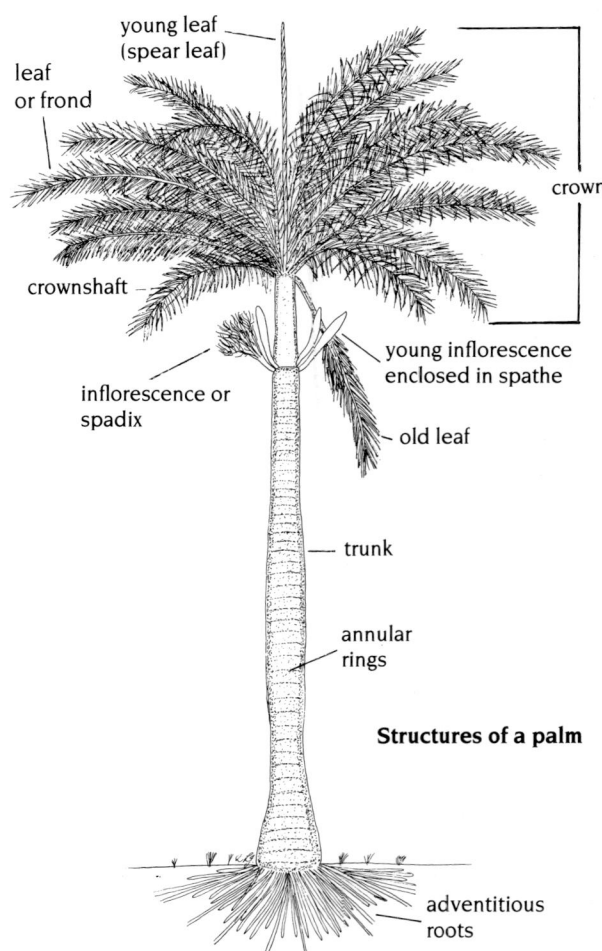

Structures of a palm

or in small groups. They range from coastal districts to inland regions and from sea level to more than 2000 m altitude.

GROWTH FEATURES

The familiar shape people associate with palms is that of a woody trunk with a distinctive rounded crown of leaves. Clumping palms may have stems in various stages of growth and present a very bushy appearance. A few palms have underground trunks, or stems so short that they appear to be trunkless. A significant group of rainforest palms are climbers which produce slender stems at intervals from an underground rhizome.

Palm trunks may be slender and resemble bamboo, or be woody or stout, tending even to be massive. In some species part of the trunk may be characteristically swollen, imparting a grotesque appearance. Ring-like scars (known as annular rings) are prominent on certain palms and these represent the point of attachment of fallen leaves. In some palms the top of the trunk is surmounted by a smooth cylinder of tightly packed leaf bases called the crownshaft. This is a useful diagnostic feature which may be greyish (*Gronophyllum ramsayi*), bright green (*Archontophoenix* species, *Roystonea* species), yellow (*Pinanga* species), ivory (*Pinanga kuhlii*) or scarlet (*Cyrtostachys renda*).

Palm leaves (which are generally called fronds) spread in a crown which tops the trunk. They may be entire (that is undivided), divided like a hand (palmate) in the fan palms, like a feather (pinnate) in the feather-leaved palms or be twice divided with characteristically shaped leaflets in the fishtail palms.

Palm flowers are small and not showy by comparison with many garden flowers. They are, however, often borne in profusion and may be quite colourful and are sometimes fragrant. Some palms flower only once in their lifetime and then die. The majority have regular flowerings throughout their life. A few species flower down the stem from each leaf axil and the whole plant or stem dies when the lowermost bunch of fruit ripens.

Palm fruits may be small and borne in profusion or large and carried in small numbers (such as the coconut). Frequently they are very colourful and are an additional decorative feature. The fruits contain one to three seeds which generally have a hard or fibrous covering.

CULTIVATING PALMS

Palms are very easy plants to grow given the basic requirements of good soil, plenty of water and some protection from hot sun when small. Mature palms are mostly sun-loving plants and should have full sunshine to achieve maximum growth. There are however some shade-loving palms which will not tolerate hot sun without bleaching or burning (e.g. *Chamaedorea* species).

Palms are generally adaptable as to soil type, however the better the soil the faster the growth and the larger the range of species which can be grown. Watering during dry periods, mulching the soil surface with organic material and applications of fertilisers and manures are all beneficial practices. Attacks by pests or diseases are generally of a minor nature.

Major types of palm leaves and their structure

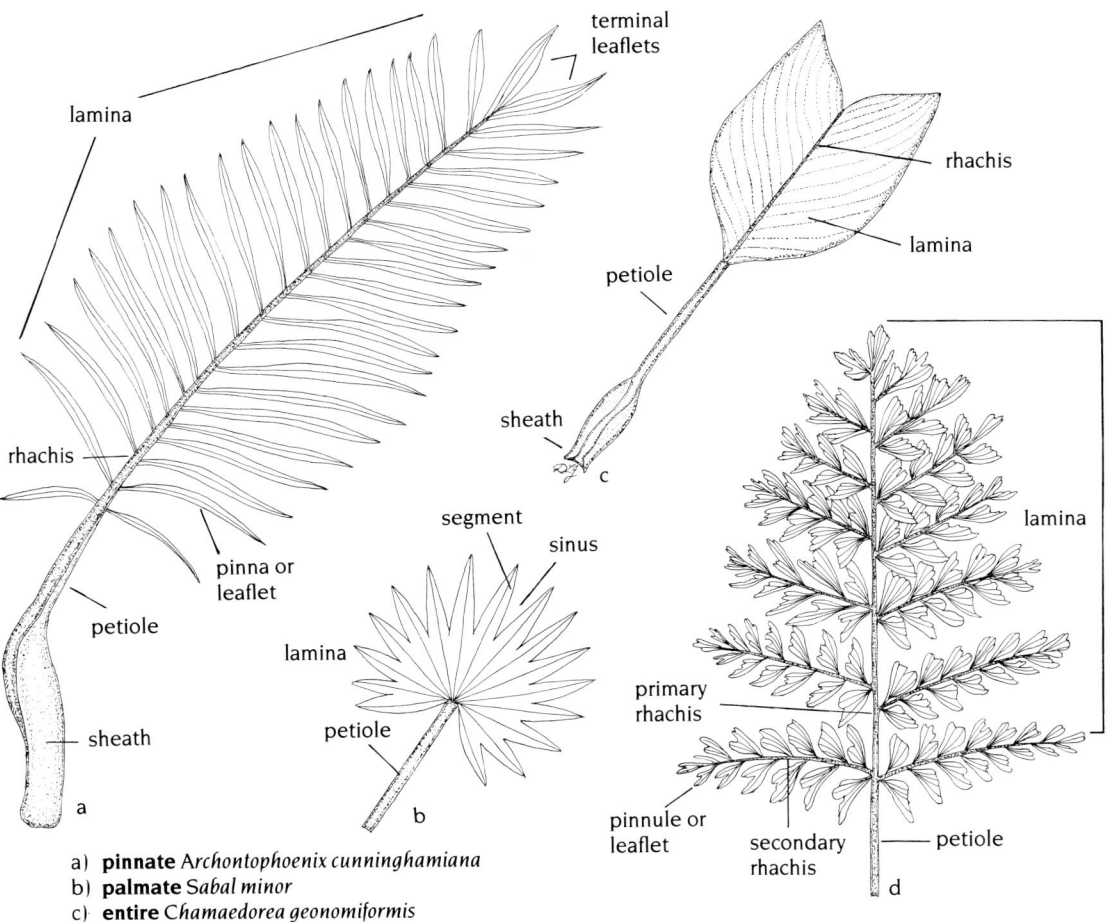

lamina

terminal
leaflets

rhachis

lamina

petiole

rhachis

pinna or
leaflet

petiole

sheath

sheath

segment

sinus

lamina

petiole

lamina

primary
rhachis

pinnule or
leaflet

secondary
rhachis

petiole

a

b

c

d

a) **pinnate** *Archontophoenix cunninghamiana*
b) **palmate** *Sabal minor*
c) **entire** *Chamaedorea geonomiformis*
d) **bipinnate** *Caryota mitis*

13

ALEXANDRA PALM

Archontophoenix alexandrae

A native palm which has become very popular in cultivation and is commonly planted in tropical and subtropical regions. It is a shapely palm with a stately silhouette, and is colourful when in flower or fruit. Plants are of suitable dimensions for home gardens. They are often planted singly as specimens but lend themselves well to group planting. Councils often use them in municipal parks, along streets, avenues, etc.

Alexandra Palm is very similar in general appearance to Bangalow Palm (see page 15) but can be distinguished at once by the white undersurface of the frond segments and the clusters of white flowers. It is much more cold sensitive than Bangalow Palm and is therefore not suited to temperate regions.

In its native state Alexandra Palm is restricted to eastern Queensland, extending from Cape York in the north to near Miriam Vale in central Queensland. It grows in large colonies along stream banks and in low-lying areas of moist soil. The extensive root systems are very important for stabilising stream banks against erosion.

Alexandra Palms can be readily propagated from fresh seed which takes one to three months to germinate.

A young plant of *Archontophoenix alexandrae* in flower.

BANGALOW PALM

Archontophoenix cunninghamiana

Bangalow Palm is one of the most familiar of our native palms for not only is it widespread and locally common but it is very popular in cultivation. Also known as Piccabeen Palm, it is renowned for its ability to withstand cyclones and other periods of strong wind, by the bending of its supple trunk.

Bangalow Palms extend from near Mackay in central Queensland to south-eastern New South Wales near Batemans Bay. They grow characteristically in extensive stands and are often prominent. The slender grey trunk may reach 25 m tall and is topped with a bright green crownshaft and a cluster of arching, feathery, dark green fronds. Prominent clusters of lilac-coloured flowers arise at the base of the crownshaft during spring and early summer and are followed by colourful groups of small, waxy, bright red fruit.

Bangalow Palms are fast growing and are planted in private gardens, parks and in commercially landscaped projects. They are excellent for group planting and develop a trunk when only about four years old. They will tolerate sun from an early age but need plenty of water. Propagation is from fresh seed which takes one to three months to germinate after sowing.

The Bangalow Palm, *Archontophoenix cunninghamiana*.

15

QUEEN PALM

Arecastrum romanzoffianum

Queen Palm is one of the most popular palms in Australia and as such is widely planted from tropical to temperate regions and from coastal to some inland districts. It is especially popular in subtropical regions (such as Queensland's Gold Coast) where it is a familiar sight in streets, public parks and private gardens.

Plants of this palm have a woody grey trunk (sometimes bulging slightly in the middle) and grow to more than 15 m tall. The rounded crown of arching, dark green fronds is graceful. Large clusters of yellow flowers (male and female on separate inflorescences) are followed by clusters of bright orange fruit. These fruit are edible but very fibrous and the taste leaves much to be desired.

Queen Palm is native to Brazil where it is prominent in coastal districts. The long botanical name is difficult to remember (and even more difficult to pronounce) and the palm is commonly sold in nurseries (although incorrectly) as *Cocos plumosus*. Occasional interesting hybrids occur between Queen Palm and Wine Palm (*Butia capitata*) where the two species grow in close proximity.

This palm does very well indoors and tolerates a fair amount of neglect. Not only does it make an excellent house plant but it is also widely used in restaurants, offices and indoor gardens in large public buildings.

Queen Palms are not fussy as to soil type but they are heavy feeders and growth is much more rapid in rich soils. They grow very well in sandy soils especially if the water table is within reach of their roots. They will also grow in clays and can be successful in limey soils although the fronds may be pale yellowish-green.

Queen Palms are very fast growing and are especially responsive to applications of nitrogenous fertilisers. Plants will tolerate sun from an early age. An open sunny situation is most successful (producing sturdy plants), however plants will also succeed in the shade of large trees eventually growing through their canopy. Large palms transplant easily with little setback. They can be grown as specimens but look especially effective when closely planted in groups. Two drawbacks of this palm are the retention of untidy dead fronds and the large clusters of fruit which, when ripe, attract noisy fruit bats and cockroaches.

Propagation of Queen Palm is from seed, which germinates easily within a few months of sowing. Seedlings are fast growing and easy to handle.

The Queen Palm (*Arecastrum romanzoffianum*), is excellent for group planting.

NATIVE ARENGA

Arenga australasica

The genus *Arenga* comprises about seventeen species of palms occurring in Asia, South-East Asia and the Pacific Islands. They are clumping or solitary palms with feathery fronds and the leaflets are notched on the margins. The trunk of a mature plant dies when the lowermost bunch of fruit is ripe. In the case of clumping species this stem is replaced by new suckers, however in those species with a solitary trunk it means the death of the plant.

Arenga australasica is restricted to Australia although it is closely related to some New Guinea species. It always grows in situations close to the coast and is often seen in wet areas behind mangroves. This species is most common in north-eastern Queensland between Bamaga (on northern Cape York Peninsula) and Innisfail. It also occurs in the Northern Territory (on the mainland near Gove and on Elcho Island) but is very rare.

Arenga australasica is a vigorous clumping palm with moderately slender stems to 20 m tall. Usually one to three stems dominate a clump and these are surrounded by a fringe of suckers. The stiff, dark green leaves spread attractively and impart a crowded impression. Plants adapt well to cultivation and can be grown in tropical and subtropical areas.

Arenga australasica.

PEACH PALM

Bactris gasipaes

Some species of palm have beautiful fruit and those of the Peach Palm are shown to perfection in the photograph. Each grows to about 8 cm across. They are not only decorative, but the dry mealy flesh may be eaten fresh or, more usually, after boiling in salt water. Palms may produce two crops a year and seedless strains are known, indicating selection and domestication by man.

This palm is widely cultivated in South America for its fruit and also its edible heart. The species has a suckering habit, and so the harvested stem is automatically replaced.

Peach Palm is virtually unknown in the wild, but is becoming widely cultivated in many countries. It thrives best in tropical regions but can also be successfully grown as far south as Brisbane. In the tropics plants can be very fast growing and like plenty of water and fertilisers.

The slender trunks of this species are liberally armed with rings of sharp spines. The crown is of arched, feathery fronds each about 3 m long and the plants have a highly ornamental appearance. They can be propagated from seed which takes about two months to germinate or by removal of suckers.

The colourful fruit of Bactris gasipaes.

BLUE HESPER PALM

Brahea armata

Palms are not generally thought of as having ornamental flowers, however the Blue Hesper Palm must be considered an exception since a flowering plant provides quite a spectacle. As the photograph shows, masses of small cream flowers are carried on long inflorescences which arch spectacularly when in flower and then droop when in fruit.

Blue Hesper Palm is native to California, USA, and grows in relatively dry situations such as on rocky slopes and gullies. Plants are generally slow growing and may live to an old age. They have a woody grey trunk, roughened with the stubs of fallen leaves. The crown is rounded and sometimes there is a skirt of dead hanging fronds. The fan-shaped powdery-blue leaves are a feature for which the species is renowned. Plants are somewhat variable as to the 'blueness' of the leaves but those growing in full sun and under tough conditions are usually the best.

Although slow growing, this species is highly ornamental and deserves to be planted on a wider scale. Plants demand freely draining well-aerated soils preferably of low fertility. Temperate to subtropical climates are most suitable and they favour an open sunny position with adequate air movement. Propagation is from seed which takes usually about three to four months to germinate.

Brahea armata in flower.

NICOBAR PALM

Bentinckia nicobarica

Bentinckia consists of just two species of palm found in India and the adjacent Nicobar Islands. They are both slender palms with a solitary trunk a prominent crownshaft and curved, feathery fronds.

Bentinckia nicobarica is restricted to the Nicobar Islands but is widely cultivated in many tropical countries. It is a fast growing, slender palm with a close superficial resemblance to the Bangalow Palm. It does, however, have a much longer crownshaft than the Bangalow Palm and very leathery leaflets which are lobed at the tip. Plants can grow to more than 20 m tall. The dense clusters of scarlet fruit are showy.

Nicobar Palm succeeds best in the tropics. It will grow in situations further south but plants are difficult to establish, slow growing and generally of poor appearance. It is a fast growing palm in the tropics and plants will tolerate sun from a very early age. They like plenty of water, mulching and regular applications of fertiliser. Being a slender palm it is well suited to planting in groups. Flowering and fruiting commences when the plants are about four years old.

Bentinckia nicobarica.

WINE PALM or JELLY PALM

Butia capitata

This is a distinctive palm which is readily recognised by its stout, woody, grey trunk (roughened by the scars left from fallen fronds) and a graceful crown of curved powdery-blue fronds. It is a native of some South American countries (particularly Brazil) where it is widespread in drier regions, sometimes growing in loose colonies.

In Australia this has proved to be an adaptable palm and plants will grow in a range of climates from the Atherton Tablelands in northeastern Queensland to Hobart in southern Tasmania. Its adaptability also embraces the changes from coastal to inland regions and indeed in inland towns the species has proved to be very hardy and the fronds are often bluer than is usually seen elsewhere.

Wine Palms are not fussy as to soil type, however they must have good drainage. An open sunny situation is essential and the palms may die if shaded too much by surrounding plants. They are generally a slow growing palm. Although unsuitable for indoor decoration they make a very decorative and hardy tub specimen.

Butia capitata is propagated from seed, however the germination is generally slow and erratic. Cracking the hard woody seed coat and soaking in warm water may hasten germination.

Butia capitata.

22

CARPENTARIA PALM

Carpentaria acuminata

An outstanding native palm from northern parts of the Northern Territory, including Arnhem Land. It has become one of the most popular palms for tropical regions and is now a very common sight in northern towns such as Cairns, Darwin and Townsville. It is very fast growing and lends itself well to group planting.

Carpentaria Palms have a slender, grey, ringed trunk topped with a bright green to greyish crownshaft and a graceful crown of curved, feathery, dark green fronds. Dense clusters of showy white flowers arise at the base of the crownshaft and are followed by large bunches of brilliant red fruit. Once plants are mature, flowering and fruiting continues almost throughout the year. Ripe fruit of this palm is a favourite item in the diet of the majestic Torres Strait Pigeon.

In its native state, Carpentaria Palms form colonies in shady forests and jungles, usually with the roots growing in wet soil. Old plants may emerge above the canopy of the forest. Fallen fruit is a common sight on the forest floor.

Plants can be successfully grown in subtropical regions, but they are much slower than in areas further north.

Carpentaria acuminata in fruit.

CLUSTERED FISHTAIL PALM

Caryota mitis

Fishtail palms are so-called because of the shape of their leaflets. They are also distinctive because their fronds are twice divided and not once divided as in the feather-leaved palms. Another interesting feature is that their stems die as the fruit on the lowest inflorescence matures. In single-trunked species this means the death of the whole plant.

Caryota mitis is a clumping palm and new suckers replace the mature stems when they die. Clumps usually consist of stems of mixed age and therefore vary in height. Individual stems grow to about 5 m tall and have fronds scattered along their length. The fronds are dark green and give the impression of lacy layers along each trunk. A well grown clump imparts a dense appearance. Small cream flowers are crowded on clustered pendulous spikes and are followed by globular, orange to deep purple fruit.

Caryota mitis is widespread in Asia extending from India to the Philippines and Indonesia (on the island of Java). It is popular in cultivation and is a familiar sight in tropical and subtropical regions. Plants will grow in full sun, but are often bleached and burnt, and have a much better appearance if given some protection. Propagation is from seed or by separation of basal suckers.

The Clustered Fishtail Palm, *Caryota mitis*.

SOLITARY FISHTAIL PALM

Caryota urens

This fishtail palm has a solitary trunk, and unlike *Caryota mitis*, the whole plant dies when the fruit ripens on the basal inflorescence. Palms can easily reach 15 m tall before this happens and may be 15 years or older.

Solitary Fishtail Palm is native to the tropics of India, Burma and Sri Lanka. It is widely cultivated in many countries and is a popular subject in Australia. Plants are well suited to tropical regions but have also proved to be adaptable and can be successful in warm temperate climates further south.

Caryota urens will tolerate sun from an early age and the palms revel in rich, loamy soils. Once established in good conditions they can be fast growing. They appreciate plenty of water and are very responsive to applications of nitrogenous fertilisers. Young plants make very attractive tub specimens, useful for indoor and foyer decorations.

Caryota urens is an imposing palm with a sturdy trunk and a fairly compact crown of spreading lacy fronds, which have drooping segments. The inflorescences may hang for more than 2.5 m, and are colourful in both flower and fruit. Propagation is solely from seed and these germinate within a few months of sowing.

The Solitary Fishtail Palm, *Caryota urens.*

METALLIC PALM

Chamaedorea metallica

The most conspicuous feature of this palm is the blue-green leaves which have a lustrous metallic sheen, particularly noticeable when they are wet. Each leaf is roughly heart-shaped and is supported in the crown by a short stalk. A crown consists of 8-10 leaves and these top a very slender, ringed trunk which resembles a section of bamboo. Plants rarely grow more than 2 m tall and are very distinctive. Flowering and fruiting inflorescences are a colourful and interesting feature.

The Metallic Palm is native to Mexico where it grows in shaded forests. Each plant is either male or female and both sexes must be growing in close proximity for fertile seed formation.

Plants of this palm are easily grown. They like good light but in a situation protected from direct sun and excess wind. Sun filtered through a canopy of foliage is ideal. Plants also appreciate loamy soil with plenty of organic mulch on the surface. Although relatively hardy to dryness these palms should be regularly watered during dry periods. Propagation is from seed which germinates readily when fresh.

The colourful inflorescence of *Chamaedorea metallica*.

BAMBOO PALM

Chamaedorea microspadix

A clumping palm which is an excellent horticultural subject because of its versatility. It is equally at home in a shaded situation in the tropics, or in a protected position in temperate regions (plants will tolerate mild frosts). As well as a garden palm, it also makes an admirable plant for indoor decoration, tolerating darkness and withstanding considerable neglect. Large plants grow well in containers and look impressive indoors.

A native of Mexico, where it grows naturally in shady forests, this species has become widely cultivated in Australia. Plants develop an open clump of slender, bamboo-like stems to 2 m tall, each stem being green and with prominent pale-coloured nodes and scattered feathery fronds. These are dull green and have regularly spaced leaflets, each drawn into a point at the apex. Clusters of small greenish flowers are followed by brilliant, orange-red globular fruit each about 1.2 cm across.

Bamboo Palm has, in Australia, often been wrongly labelled as *Chamaedorea erumpens*, a species which appears to be rarely cultivated. It is also superficially similar to *Chamaedorea costaricana* from Costa Rica. This species which is also grown in Australia (common in Royal Botanic Gardens, Sydney) is very vigorous and has black fruit.

The Bamboo Palm, *Chamaedorea microspadix*.

27

EUROPEAN FAN PALM

Chamaerops humilis

Shallow, often stony soils are the preferred habitat of this tough Fan Palm. As the common name suggests it occurs in some countries of Europe (actually the Mediterranean area of southern Europe including Spain, Italy and Portugal) and in northern Africa (Morocco, Libya, etc.). It is found in a variety of habitats from coastal districts (where it grows on beaches and rocky cliffs) to inland gorges and mountains, where snow may fall in winter. It often grows in colonies.

European Fan Palm is somewhat variable in its growth habit. Commonly it is a suckering palm forming spreading clumps with a few dominant stems to 3 m tall, these being surrounded by shorter, juvenile growth. In another form, the plants do not sucker but develop a single, relatively slender trunk to 4 m or 5 m tall. A dwarf form is also known which is virtually trunkless.

In its native state various parts of this palm may be used by people for a range of purposes. Vegetable Horsehair or African Hair is the name given to the black leaf fibres which are used as a substitute for horsehair in upholstery or for weaving into carpets. The leaves can also be shredded for their fibres or woven into hats, baskets and other utensils. The young suckers are collected in some countries and eaten after cooking.

The photograph shows a typical clump of European Fan Palms. The sturdy dark trunks (which are often curved) are covered with the woody bases of fallen fronds, and each is topped with a rounded crown which may be dark green or grey-green. Each frond has a slender spiny petiole and a blade which is deeply divided into stiff segments. A plant is either male or female and the small flowers are produced in short, dense fleshy clusters from among the leaf stalks. The male flowers are a brighter yellow than the females and have prominent stamens. The fruit, which are 1-2 cm across, are variable in shape (round to oblong) and in colour (yellow to orange or brown).

European Fan Palm is a hardy species valuable for cultivation, since it will survive a wide range of climates (tropical to temperate; coastal to inland) and soil types including those which are very shallow and infertile. It will not, however, tolerate waterlogged soils. Plants are hardy to severe frosts and once established will withstand neglect and dryness. An open, sunny position is most suitable.

The European Fan Palm, *Chamaerops humilis.*

GOLDEN CANE PALM or BUTTERFLY PALM

Chrysalidocarpus lutescens

The genus *Chrysalidocarpus* is restricted entirely to Madagascar and a few adjacent islands. It is a group of about twenty species of palms (some clumping, some solitary) which have attractive, feathery crowns.

The most common species grown in Australia is *Chrysalidocarpus lutescens*. This species is a clumping palm, prized for its slender golden-yellow stems and the appealingly twisted, feathery fronds which are also in yellowish hues. These features have given rise to the apt vernacular of Golden Cane Palm. It is often sold by nurseries (erroneously) as *Areca lutescens*.

Plants of this palm are commonly seen in tropical and subtropical parks and gardens, but the species is also adaptable to temperate regions and large, old specimens are known from as far south as Melbourne. Plants form a dense clump to ground level and are excellent for screening purposes. Some people enhance the beauty of the mature stems by pruning off all suckers as they emerge. This imparts a very different appearance to the plant.

Golden Cane Palm is excellent for indoor decoration and plants in tubs are widely used for this purpose. Seed takes about six months to germinate. The species can also be propagated by the removal of suckers.

A large clump of *Chrysalidocarpus lutescens*.

GUADELOUPE FAN PALM

Coccothrinax dussiana

The genus *Coccothrinax* contains about twenty species of interesting fan palms occurring mainly in the West Indies and extending to Florida. All are slender palms with a solitary trunk and have a graceful habit. They are uncommonly grown in Australia, although they are quite attractive and deserve to be more widely known.

Coccothrinax dussiana is native to Guadeloupe and grows naturally in shaded coastal forests in soils containing limestone. It is a very graceful palm with a slender trunk to about 8 m tall. This trunk is naked except in the crown where it is thickly covered with brown fibres. The fan-shaped leaves are bright green on the upper surface and silvery-white beneath. They are held stiffly in the crown, although older leaves may hang. Short, slender inflorescences arise among the leaves and bear creamy-yellow flowers. These are followed by clusters of small, fleshy, purple-black fruit.

Coccothrinax dussiana is a slow growing palm but is worth waiting for. It grows well in tropical and subtropical regions in a partially protected situation. Soil drainage must be unimpeded and a dressing of lime may be beneficial. Young plants are excellent container subjects.

Coccothrinax dussiana.

COCONUT PALM

Cocos nucifera

The Coconut Palm is regarded as the jewel of the tropics and it is undoubtedly the most economically important palm to mankind. More than 13 million people are directly or indirectly involved with coconut products and Coconut Palms are widely planted in the tropical regions of the world. They are an important economic crop for many small countries, particularly in the Pacific region. In the South Pacific, for example, it is estimated that about 400 000 people depend entirely on the coconut for their livelihood. World production is about 3000 million nuts annually and these are produced from groves totalling more than four million hectares. The major producers are the Philippines, India and Indonesia.

The range of uses to which various parts of the Coconut Palm can be put is truly amazing. Every part can be used in some way. The major use of the nut is for oil extraction from the dried meat (copra). Coconut oil is a major component of vegetable oils used for the production of margarine, dressing, soap, shampoo etc. It makes up about 20 per cent of all vegetable oils used in the world. Coconut meat can be cooked in more than a hundred different dishes or eaten raw or shredded and dried. The water of a green coconut makes a refreshing drink or it can be blended with the meat to make coconut milk,

cream or jam. The heart (cabbage) of fallen palms can be eaten and the sap of the inflorescence can be converted to palm sugar or alcoholic drinks.

Coconut Palms are commonly associated with the white beaches fringing tropical islands and it is here that they are at their best. As well as being attractive they have an unparalleled ability to add a tropical flavour to a beach resort and are therefore widely planted as ornamentals by landscape gardeners in developed countries.

Coconut Palms are very easily grown in tropical areas but are much more difficult in subtropical climates. They rarely fruit in areas with a cold winter and may be killed by severe cold snaps. A tropical regime is necessary for continued fruit production with a uniform temperature range throughout the year (a mean of 20°C) and a well distributed annual rainfall of about 1000 mm per annum. Plants need well drained soil and will thrive if their roots can tap ground water. They will grow inland in tropical regions but are not as successful as on the coast.

The Coconut Palm has numerous horticultural cultivars varying from dwarf to tall growing and bearing fruit in a range of sizes, colours and shapes.

A clump of Coconut Palms (*Cocos nucifera*).
Photo Bruce Gray

SEALING WAX PALM or MAHARAJAH PALM

Cyrtostachys renda

Without doubt this is one of the most colourful of all palms. The scarlet leaf bases, petioles and main leaf stalk provide a brilliant splash of colour which can be seen from a distance. The effect is enhanced by the clumping habit.

Sealing Wax Palm is unfortunately very tropical in its requirements and in Australia is suited only to northern towns such as Cairns and Darwin. It deserves to be mass-planted in these regions in both public and private gardens.

The palm is native to Malaysia and grows in near coastal swamps. Visitors to Malaysia and Singapore can readily appreciate the beauty of this palm for it is widely planted as an ornamental in towns, streets and parks.

Trunks of this palm are held in a stiffly erect manner and are slender (about 8 cm across) with distinct, pale rings. The crowns are generally small with the fronds arching and the leaflets erect or obliquely erect. Flower spikes are reddish with small green flowers which are followed by black fruit.

Propagation of the Sealing Wax Palm can be from seed or by removal of suckers. The latter method is favoured because such plants develop a colourful crownshaft within a short period compared to seedlings.

The beautiful crownshafts of the Sealing Wax Palm (*Cyrtostachys renda*).
Photo Dennis Hundscheidt

AMERICAN OIL PALM

Elaeis guineensis

An ornamental palm from central and tropical west Africa which has become of commercial significance for the valuable oils which can be extracted from its fruit pulp and the seeds. These oils are used in industrialised countries for the manufacture of margarine, detergents and cosmetics and as a valuable lubricant. Oil Palm plantations are now established in various countries including Indonesia, Malaysia, New Guinea, Nigeria and parts of Central and South America. Superior strains have been selected to give a greater yield of oil and these plants are propagated by tissue culture.

Elaeis guineensis is a stately palm which is excellent for parkland planting. Specimens develop a large rounded crown of feathery fronds, each to 5 m long. These top a woody trunk (to 18 m tall), which is roughened with the bases of fallen fronds. Male and female flowers are borne in separate inflorescences (each very distinctive) arising in the bases of the fronds. The black fruit is carried in densely congested heads.

Oil Palms are suitable for tropical and subtropical regions, in coastal as well as inland districts. They require sunny conditions, freely draining soil and plenty of water. Plants are fairly slow growing. Seed germinates erratically.

The American Oil Palm, Elaeis guineensis.

NORTHERN KENTIA PALM

Gronophyllum ramsayi

A unique native palm endemic to the Northern Territory. It grows in colonies and is known from a few areas on northern parts of the mainland (including Arnhem Land), as well as Croker and Melville Islands off the coast. In some areas (such as around Murganella) the Northern Kentia is extremely common and covers extensive areas, sometimes growing in almost pure stands. It favours infertile sandy soils and seems to proliferate where ground water is present. Seedlings commonly cover the ground under mature plants.

This palm was important to the Aborigines who lived and hunted in its habitat. To them the heart was a very tasty delicacy and baskets were fashioned from the base of fallen fronds. The fronds were probably used to construct shelters.

Northern Kentia is a majestic palm with a distinctive appearance. The solid grey trunk is topped by a prominent crownshaft and a round crown of greyish feathery fronds. Each frond curves backwards stiffly and has upright leaflets. Pendulous clusters carry male or female flowers (both strongly lemon-scented) and the females are followed by brilliant red, waxy fruit.

Northern Kentia Palms have unfortunately proved to be slow growing and are difficult to establish successfully.

The Northern Kentia Palm, *Gronophyllum ramsayi*.

GULUBIA PALM

Gulubia costata

Gulubia consists of nine species of palms found in Indonesia, Fiji, New Hebrides, Solomon Islands, New Guinea and Australia. They are tall slender palms which usually grow in colonies and tower above the surrounding vegetation. They commonly occur around streams or swampy depressions in rainforests.

Gulubia costata occurs in New Guinea and Australia. It is very widespread and common in the lowlands of New Guinea but in Australia is restricted to a few colonies on the northern part of Cape York Peninsula. The tops of the palms are visible above the forest canopies and this enables the colonies to be located easily. Often there is very little or no plant growth on the ground under the colonies; even very few palm seedlings.

Gulubia Palms may grow more than 30 m tall and have a very slender trunk. Their drooping leaflets are a most distinctive feature; these hang along the whole length of the spreading, feathery fronds. Large clusters of deep maroon fruit are showy.

Gulubia costata is suited only to the tropics. Plants have proved to be very sensitive to cold and will quickly die in an unsuitable climate. They are very fast growing, especially if regularly watered and mulched.

Gulubia costata. Photo Bruce Gray

KENTIA PALM
or THATCH PALM

Howea forsteriana

It is quite astounding to consider how familiar this palm has become in dozens of countries around the world, and yet its natural distribution is restricted entirely to the tiny oceanic mass of Lord Howe Island which is found to the east of Australia. It is one of the best indoor palms available anywhere, and is in such demand that a seedling export industry has been established on the island. Ripe seeds are collected annually by the local people, germinated in a nursery on the island and packed in polystyrene boxes before being air-freighted to their destination.

Plants are renowned for their graceful habit and are unexcelled in their tolerance of indoor conditions, including poor light, a dry atmosphere and neglect. They are also a beautiful garden palm with their slender grey trunk and graceful crown of dark green, drooping fronds. Plants are particularly well suited to coastal gardens and can be grown as far south as Melbourne. Some people plant them as specimens but they are better suited to group planting, particularly in groups of mixed age.

Seeds of Kentia Palm hang on strings about 1 m long and take three to four years to ripen. They colour very slowly eventually becoming bright red when fully ripe. Seedlings may take one to three years to appear after sowing.

CURLY PALM
or SENTRY PALM

Howea belmoreana

This palm is also native to Lord Howe Island, but unlike its famous relative, the Kentia Palm (*Howea forsteriana*), it is relatively uncommon in cultivation. While it is still an excellent little palm with unique features, it lacks the grace of its more salubrious relative and (more importantly) it does not perform as well when grown indoors.

Curly Palm gains its common name from its appealing crown of fronds, each of which arches strongly from the trunk. The stiff, bright green leaflets are held erect, adding to the effect. Slender pendulous inflorescences (to 1.5 m long) are densely covered with small cream flowers. Egg-shaped fruit ripen over two to four years eventually becoming brownish-red.

Odd mature plants of Curly Palm can be seen in some inner suburbs of Sydney. Its neat habit and relatively small size, make it an excellent palm for gardens where room is limited. Plants are generally slow growing and need protection when small. They are not fussy as to soil type providing the drainage is free and unimpeded. Watering and mulches assist growth. Propagation is from seed which may take one to three years to germinate.

A mixed stand of Curly Palm (*Howea belmoreana*)
and Kentia Palm (*Howea forsteriana*). The Curly
Palms have brighter green crowns.

BOTTLE PALM

Hyophorbe lagenicaulis

It is easy to understand why this species is called the Bottle Palm, because the base of the trunk is greatly swollen and then tapers upwards to the crown. This feature is well illustrated in the photograph, which is of a fairly young specimen.

The trunk is prominently ringed and becomes grey and woody in old specimens. The crown surprisingly consists of only four to six fronds, arising above a smooth green crownshaft. Each frond (to 2 m long), arches stiffly, and is divided into numerous slender, partially erect segments. Stiff inflorescences arise at the base of the crownshaft and carry small cream flowers. These are followed by round to oblong yellow-black fruit each about 2 cm long.

Bottle Palm is native to a single island in the Mascarene group of islands off Mauritius. It has become extremely rare and less than twenty plants are known in its natural state. Fortunately it has become well entrenched in cultivation and is now widely grown in many tropical countries. Plants are very sensitive to cold and while they can succeed in a warm situation in the subtropics, they are best suited to zones further north. They are slow growing and require a sunny situation. Seed takes about six to eight months to germinate.

The well named Bottle Palm, *Hyophorbe lagenicaulis.*

SPINDLE PALM

Hyophorbe verschaffeltii

Like the Bottle Palm, this species takes its common name from the spindle-shaped trunk, which is thickest in the middle and tapers to each end. It also is native to the Mascarene Island group, this time the island of Rodriquez.

Spindle Palm grows to about 5 m tall and the trunk is topped with a prominent bright green crownshaft which bulges at the base. The crown consists of six to ten feathery dark green fronds which arch in a most attractive manner. Several inflorescences appear at the base of the crownshaft and before unfolding these are carried in unusual curved horn-like spathes. Stiff, much-branched inflorescences carry small flowers and then masses of large, waxy, bright red fruit.

Spindle Palm is popular in tropical regions and its distinctive shape makes it readily recognisable. It is more cold tolerant than Bottle Palm and is also familiar in subtropical parks and gardens. There are some fine specimens in Brisbane. Plants are slow growing and require a sunny situation from an early age. Good drainage is essential, and they like watering during dry periods. Seed takes about six months to germinate.

The Spindle Palm in flower (*Hyophorbe verschaffeltii*).

UMBRELLA PALM or BIG MOUNTAIN PALM

Hedyscepe canterburyana

This is another unique palm found only on Lord Howe Island (see also Kentia Palm and Curly Palm). It is not usually seen by general visitors to the island as it is restricted to the mountains between 400 m and 800 m altitude. However those intrepid folk who undertake the mountain walk will certainly notice this unusual palm, for it is common both in the good forests as well as the stunted forests of higher levels.

Umbrella Palm is a sturdy species with a prominently ringed green or grey trunk topped with a stout, bluish-green crownshaft and a sparse crown of stiff fronds. These are curved (often partially twisted) and have numerous leaflets which are held stiffly erect. Coarse clusters of relatively large greenish-white flowers arise at the base of the crownshaft and are followed by fat brownish fruit about 3 cm long. These may take three to four years to ripen.

Despite its excellent ornamental appearance this palm is rarely grown. Plants are extremely slow growing and rather stringent in their requirements of coolness, shade and plenty of moisture. They also like organically-rich, loamy soil which drains freely after watering. Seeds are slow to germinate, seedlings taking up to twelve months to appear.

The Umbrella Palm (*Hedyscepe canterburyana*) on Mt Gower, Lord Howe Island.

CHILEAN WINE PALM or COQUITO PALM

Jubaea chilensis

An eye-catching palm made noticeable by its massive woody trunk which is patterned by the scars from fallen leaves. The trunk may grow to 20 m tall and is more than 1m thick. In its native country of Chile these magnificent palms were once cut down to collect their sugary sap, which was then either fermented into wine or boiled to produce the local delicacy known as palm honey. The palms are now fully protected in their native state and felling is illegal.

Jubaea chilensis is a very slow growing palm and the specimens in our botanic gardens are the result of many years' growth. A temperate climate is most suitable for them and they are quite hardy to frosts. Regular watering is necessary during dry periods. Plants do not seem to be especially responsive to fertiliser applications.

As well as its massive trunk, this palm has a rounded crown of slender feathery fronds which have a paler undersurface. The inflorescences bear purple flowers (separate male and female) and then pale yellow fruit about 5 cm long, which resemble miniature coconuts. The seed of these is edible. Propagation of this palm is from seed which may take six to twelve months to germinate.

The very sturdy *Jubaea chilensis*.

FAN PALM

Licuala grandis

An outstanding ornamental palm which is prized for its wonderfully symmetrical, fan-shaped leaves. These are about 1m across, attractively pleated and with toothed margins. They are normally a fresh, bright green in colour. The leaves are closely arranged in the crown and present a very tropical appearance.

Licuala grandis is essentially a palm for the tropics, although specimens can be successfully nurtured in warm coastal districts of the sub-tropics. Plants like good light and will grow in full sun if they are kept moist. They develop a very slender grey trunk to about 3 m tall. Long pendulous spikes are colourful when covered with masses of small brilliant orange-red fruit.

Fan Palm makes an excellent, long-lasting tub plant and can be used for indoor decoration. A friable, well-drained, organically-rich potting mix is necessary. Young plants are fairly slow growing and should not be overpotted. They are also very sensitive to drying of the root system.

A native of the New Hebrides, this species has become firmly entrenched in horticulture. It can be readily propagated from seed which takes three to five months to germinate.

Licuala grandis . Photo Chris Goudey

NATIVE FAN PALM

Licuala ramsayi

A spectacular palm from north-eastern Queensland where it is found in lowland districts not too far from the coast. It grows in rainforests along stream banks subject to inundation and in swampy areas. It may form extensive pure colonies and the dark conditions created by the overlapping leaves reduce the undergrowth to a minimum. When the sun is shining overhead these fronds create a beautiful symmetrical pattern. The large fronds move and creak in the slightest breeze and to sleep under a canopy of these palms is quite an experience.

Plants of the Native Fan Palm develop a slender woody trunk to about 10 m tall. This is topped by the crown of spectacular rounded leaves which have closely placed segments and irregularly toothed margins. Large clusters of white flowers are quite noticeable among the leaves and are followed by brilliant orange-red fruit.

Licuala ramsayi is an easy palm to cultivate but plants are very slow growing. The fronds of young palms have widely spaced segments and are very different in appearance to mature leaves. Plants need a warm sheltered position in loamy soil. They like plenty of moisture and mulching of the soil surface is beneficial.

Leaf silhouettes in a colony of Fan Palms (*Licuala ramsayi*).

BLUE LATAN PALM

Latania loddigesii

The genus *Latania* consists of three species of palms, all being endemic to the Mascarene Islands. Each species is basically similar in appearance to the others and can usually be distinguished by the colouration of the leaves and petioles and details of that part of the leaf where the stalk ends in the blade. Seedlings of each species often have a more intense colouration than in the adults.

All three species have slender grey ringed trunks and a compact, dense crown of stiffly curved fan-shaped leaves. The base of each leaf stalk is characteristically split and each half sheaths the trunk. This feature is well illustrated in the colour plate. The leaf blades are deeply divided into stiff segments and have a prominent grey powdery, or waxy, coating on the undersurface. Clusters of yellowish flowers arise among the leaves and are followed by fairly large pale green to brown fruit, which ripen slowly.

The Blue Latan Palm is a very slow growing species but its highly ornamental appearance is worth waiting for. Plants will grow in tropical, subtropical and warm temperate regions but are not suited to colder climates. They need well-drained soil and a sunny position. Once established, the plants are hardy to dry periods.

The crown of a Blue Latan Palm (*Latania loddigesii*).

46

CHINESE FAN PALM

Livistona chinensis

A popular palm valued for the slender drooping segments of its fronds. Collectively these impart a weeping appearance to the crown. The fronds have a slender stalk and a fan-shaped, deeply divided blade which is commonly yellowish-green. Clusters of attractive yellow flowers arise within the crown and are followed by ovoid bluish fruit about 2.5 cm across.

Chinese Fan Palm is native to Japan, the Ryukyu Islands and parts of Taiwan and China. It is very commonly planted in Australia and grows particularly well in temperate and subtropical climates. Growth is slow but plants develop a spreading crown from an early age. They will grow in shady or sunny situations but produce a more colourful crown in brighter light. Plants are tolerant of poor soil but improve with applications of fertiliser. Cultivated specimens in excess of 6 m tall are rare.

The genus *Livistona* consists of about twenty-eight species of Fan Palm with the majority occurring in Australia. Others are known from Asia, Malaysia, the Philippines and New Guinea. Relatively few exotic species are cultivated in Australia. Propagation is from seed which germinates readily.

Livistona chinensis. Photo Chris Goudey

CABBAGE PALM or FAN PALM

Livistona australis

The common name of Cabbage Palm originated with the early Australian settlers, who ate the heart of the crown (either cooked or raw) and noted its similarity to the taste of cabbage. This palm achieved considerable familiarity with these pioneers who put parts of it to various uses. In the hot climate hats are of the utmost importance and the large leaves of Cabbage Palm were ideal for this purpose. The fronds were collected, immersed in boiling water and allowed to dry. The fibres were then stripped, shredded and plaited into Cabbage Tree hats which were a good local substitute for the imported Panama hat. The leaves were also used to make baskets. The sturdy trunks were hollowed by the farmers as feed troughs for their animals or split and used to construct slab huts. Walking sticks and inlays used to decorate furniture were made from the attractively marked inner wood of the trunk.

Cabbage Palms were also of importance to the Aborigines who ate the young leaves, as well as the cabbage. Fibres from the mature leaves were used to make nets and fishing lines, and the leaves covered the roofs of their shelters. The hard wood of the outer trunk was excellent for spear heads.

Cabbage Palms are endemic to Australia and are distributed from Fraser Island in south-eastern Queensland through eastern New South Wales and there are three isolated colonies in eastern Victoria. This makes it the most southerly growing palm in Australia. A range of habitats are occupied but the species seems to favour rainforests and moist localities such as along the banks of watercourses. It is often noticeable in low-lying swampy situations where it may form congested colonies which are almost pure stands.

Cabbage Palms have a single grey woody trunk and grow to more than 30 m tall. The crown is characteristically rounded and consists of large fan-shaped fronds (divided into numerous, slender segments) with the lower (older) fronds dead or dying and turning grey-brown. Healthy fronds are a bright shiny green and the segments have drooping tips. During September – October, large (to 1 m long) much-branched panicles of cream to white flowers become conspicuous in the leafy crown. They are followed by black globular fruit which are about 1.5 cm across and very hard.

Cabbage Palms are quite popular in cultivation and are a familiar sight in municipal parks. They will grow readily in a range of soils and like plenty of moisture. Propagation is by seed which germinates readily if freshly sown.

A colony of *Livistona australis*.

KIMBERLEY FAN PALM

Livistona eastonii

The photograph depicts a colony of this elegant palm early in the wet season. The plants are in a flush of growth producing new fronds while there is sufficient water to grow. The old fronds are hanging as a skirt below the crown.

The climate where this palm grows naturally is strongly seasonal. The wet season occurs from December to March and the area is deluged by heavy rain which often accompanies cyclones. From April onwards the area dries out and very little rain falls until the next wet season. The climate becomes progressively hotter, reaching a peak in October – November. By June all of the annual grasses and herbs have died back and the groundcover is brown. Fires occur regularly each dry season and these burn all of the dead fronds (and frequently most of the live ones) from the crown of the palm. The palms are quite resistant to these fires and recover within a short period.

Kimberley Fan Palm is restricted to the Kimberley region of northern Western Australia. It grows in extensive colonies in open forests on gravelly or laterite soils. The colonies consist of all age groups and seedlings are common. Old plants (to 8 m tall) may tower above the others.

This palm was discovered relatively recently in Australia and was described by C. A. Gardner in 1923. Gardner was the Government Botanist in Western Australia from 1929 to 1960 and he named the palm in honour of its discoverer, W. R. Easton. Easton was a contract surveyor who found the palm while leading the Western Australian Government sponsored Kimberley Exploration Expedition in 1921.

Livistona eastonii is a very slender palm, the woody trunk of which is patterned with a spiral of thick, persistent leaf bases. The fronds arch in a fairly sparse crown. They are glaucous when young but mature to shiny green or yellowish-green. The blade of each frond is conspicuously folded and deeply divided into slender segments. The petiole is slender and has a few thorns scattered along its margins. Stiff, fairly short panicles bear small cream flowers and these are followed by small globular black fruit.

Kimberley Fan Palm is rarely cultivated and may be a difficult species to grow. Plants have proved to be very slow growing. They are best suited to tropical regions with a drier climate (such as Darwin). Fresh seed takes about three months to germinate.

A colony of *Livistona eastonii* in the Kimberley
region, WA. Photo Clyde Dunlop

SAND PALM

Livistona humilis

Visitors to northern regions of the Northern Territory cannot fail to notice this small, slender palm. It dominates some open forests, growing in extensive colonies and sometimes almost in congested patches. It is still prominent very close to Darwin, and can be seen beside both the Stuart and Arnhem highways. It commonly grows in sandy soils (hence the common name) but may also occur in laterites.

The botanical epithet 'humilis' means of low stature, and this species is certainly small when compared with some other members of the genus. Most *Livistona humilis* plants seen are 1 — 3 m tall but occasionally old specimens in excess of 5 m are encountered. Plants have a very slender trunk (about 10 cm thick) and this is usually black and roughened from the bases of fallen fronds. The rounded crown is fairly dense and consists of fan-shaped fronds each about 1 m long. These have a slender petiole margined with prickles, and a bright shiny green blade which is divided into numerous, stiff segments.

Individual plants of Sand Palm are either male or female and each type has a different inflorescence which arches well clear of the fronds. Those on the male plants are fairly broad and prominently branched while the females are slender and with few branches. The tiny flowers are pale to bright yellow and on the female plants, these are followed by clusters of ovoid black fruit each about 1.5 cm long. These fruit may hang on the plants for a couple of months.

Sand Palm is restricted to northern parts of the Northern Territory but is locally common. Bushfires occur almost annually in the habitat where it grows and the palm is well adapted to survive. In severe fires the crown may be completely destroyed but the important apical meristem is well protected by the fibrous trunk. New fronds are produced within two weeks of a fire and in a few months its effects have been hidden by a fresh green crown.

Sand Palm was utilised by the Aborigines during the months of the wet season when they ate the heart. It is cultivated as an ornamental on a limited scale in Darwin, however plants are very slow growing and not generally amenable. Seed usually takes six to twelve months to germinate.

A colony of *Livistona humilis*.

CENTRAL AUSTRALIAN CABBAGE PALM

Livistona mariae

Palms are usually associated with rainforests or moist climates and it is remarkable to find this species surviving in the hostile arid climate of Central Australia where it is separated from any other species of palm by more than 1000 km. Obviously the palm is a relict, surviving from a much moister climate which is now long gone. The species has only just survived, for it is now restricted to permanent water along the Finke River and its tributaries. In these gorges, pools, springs and areas of soakage supply the moisture essential for the survival of the species. The photograph clearly shows the palms huddled around their oasis in a hostile and forbidding climate.

Central Australian Cabbage Palm is a majestic species which grows in colonies. The woody trunk may reach 20 m or more tall and about 30 cm across, with a swollen base. It is dark grey and prominently ringed. The crown of fan-shaped fronds is large, rounded and moderately dense. Each frond has a stout petiole about 2 m long which is spiny at the base, and a large leathery blade of similar length. This is shiny green on the upper surface and greyish beneath from a thick coating of wax. The slender segments are twice divided and droop at the tips. Panicles of pale yellow flowers about 1 m long are borne among the fronds and are followed by clusters of globular black fruit about 2 cm across.

Some Aboriginal tribes of Central Australia knew of this palm and collected and ate the cabbage and very young leaves. It was first seen by white men in the 1850s and was officially described by Baron Ferdinand von Mueller in 1878. Despite its rarity this palm is known to thousands of people because Palm Valley is now a famous visiting point in Central Australia for tourists from all countries.

Livistona mariae has attracted the attention of horticulturists because of its rarity, and it has been planted in a number of countries as well as in its native Australia. Seedlings develop colourful reddish leaves and have numerous prickles on the margins of the segments. Plants grow best in a dry warm climate and need plenty of water. They are tolerant of full sun when quite small. The seeds take about four to eight months to germinate and seedlings are generally slow growing.

Livistona mariae in Palm Valley, Central Australia.
Photo Jim Willis

RIGID FAN PALM

Livistona rigida

A native palm from inland areas of northern Queensland and the Northern Territory. Its stronghold in Queensland is the Gregory River and its tributaries, where it grows in extensive stands along the banks (often becoming inundated during floods). The soils in this vicinity are heavy clays and silty alluvium. In the Northern Territory the same species occurs on the fringes of the springs at Mataranka, growing on limestone.

Rigid Fan Palm is well named for its stiff imposing appearance. Plants develop a fairly woody grey to brown trunk which often has noticeable growth rings. The crown is fairly open and consists of fan-shaped fronds about 4 m long, each with a stiff dull blade which is bluish-green to yellowish-green. The tips of the segments do not droop as they do in many other fan palms. The leaves of young plants often have reddish tinges. Dense clusters of small yellowish flowers are borne within the crown and are followed by hard globular black fruit about 2 cm across.

Rigid Fan Palm is a tough species for tropical towns and inland regions which do not experience heavy frosts. Plants can be fast growing and appreciate plenty of water.

Livistona rigida.

56

WEDDING PALM

Microcoelum weddellianum

Young plants of this palm are valued for their lustrous dark green fronds which arch from the crown in a most appealing manner. Plants at this stage of growth are popular for indoor decoration and they perform very well in this role. They will tolerate quite dark conditions and some neglect. Scale insects and mealy bugs may become problems pests.

This palm adapts very well to pot culture and may be very long-lived. Plants can be potted back into the same size container for many years, providing there is some root pruning and replenishment of the potting mix with fresh compost.

Microcoelum weddellianum is a graceful, slow growing palm which develops a slender grey ringed trunk to about 3 m tall. The crown on older plants is rounded with the arching fronds being about 1 m long. Inflorescences nearly as long as the leaves bear bright yellow flowers and these are followed by brownish fruit which resemble miniature coconuts.

Wedding Palm is native to Brazil and can be grown outdoors in subtropical and warm temperate gardens. For best appearance plants should have a partially protected situation. They also like heavy mulching of the soil surface and watering during dry periods. Propagation is from seed which takes two to four months to germinate.

Microcoelum weddellianum.

MANGROVE PALM or NIPAH PALM

Nypa fruticans

This is a very widely distributed palm which grows in a remarkably specialised habitat. It favours the soft mud of tidal creeks, rivers and estuaries at a point where the water is brackish and can sometimes be fresh. Tidal fluctuations result in the frond bases and rhizomes being regularly covered and uncovered by water. The palm is a clumping species and commonly grows in colonies which vary from narrow strips fringing creeks to extensive colonies in low-lying ground. It is distributed in tropical parts of Asia, South-East Asia and various Pacific Islands to northern Australia (Queensland and the Northern Territory).

The trunks of the Mangrove Palm are completely buried in mud. They branch freely, always by a forking process at the apex and this results in two equal branches. The fronds, which may grow to 9 m long, arise in a crown at the apex of each trunk. Air spaces in the leaf stems aid bouyancy. The leaves are pinnately divided with about 100 leaflets on each frond. These are each dark green on the upper surface and powdery-white beneath. A most unusual flowering structure (1-2 m long) arises directly from the rhizome. This consists of a central globular head (the female flowers) subtended by bright yellow catkins of male flowers all nestled among papery bracts at the end of a stout stalk. The male flowers are short-lasting and the female head

develops into a woody structure containing the fruit. The fruit float on sea water and are distributed by ocean currents.

Nipah Palm is a valuable palm that is widely used by the local people wherever it grows. The stiff fronds are excellent for thatching and may also be woven into wall partitions. Young seeds are edible and are reportedly tasty. If the developing inflorescence is cut, a sugary sap issues in good quantity from the cut surface. This can be collected and converted into sugar or alcohol. The Nipa huts of the Philippines are constructed largely or entirely of palm products most of which originate from the Nipah Palm.

As may be expected from its specialised habitat, *Nypa fruticans* is not an easy palm to grow. It has, however, been cultivated successfully and needs an abundance of water. The water need not be brackish, as evidenced by its successful cultivation in a fresh water swamp in the Bogor Botanic Gardens, and also in a tropical glasshouse at the Royal Botanic Gardens, Kew, England. Plants are very sensitive to cold and are generally slow growing.

A clump of the Mangrove Palm, *Nypa fruticans*.

IVORY CANE PALM

Pinanga kuhlii

Species of *Pinanga* are amongst the most beautiful of tropical palms. They are prized for their graceful habit and neat crown of feathery fronds. The stems are slender and bamboo-like with prominent growth rings. The fronds often have widely spaced leaflets (some species have entire fronds) which may be variable in shape. Frequently the inflorescence and fruit are of bright contrasting colours and provide a decorative conversation piece.

The genus consists of about 120 species which are distributed in Asia, South China, South-East Asia and extend to New Guinea. They are mostly small to medium-sized palms which grow in shady rainforests and jungles. A few species are robust and their crowns may emerge above the forest canopy and grow in sunlight. Clumping as well as solitary species are known within the genus and some may even be trunk-less. An appealing feature on some species of *Pinanga* is that the leaves may be attractively mottled and blotched. This is often noticeable on young plants.

Unfortunately most species of *Pinanga* are very sensitive to cold weather and are therefore best regarded as palms for tropical regions. Relatively few hardy species will grow as far south as Brisbane and even these need a sheltered location.

Pinanga kuhlii is one species which can be grown in subtropical regions. It is commonly known as the Ivory Cane Palm because its stems have a prominent crownshaft which is ivory or bone-coloured. It is a clumping palm with a dense habit of growth and attractive fronds which have broad well-separated leaflets. The fronds are held obliquely erect and are an appealing bright green. They arise in a spreading crown from each stem. The stems, which may grow to 5 m tall, are only about 3 cm thick and have broad pale growth rings. Inflorescences arise from the base of the crownshaft and bear prominent yellowish-cream flowers. At fruiting time the egg-shaped dark red fruit contrast pleasantly with the pink inflorescence stalks to provide a colourful display.

Ivory Cane Palm, which is native to Indonesia, is deservedly popular in cultivation. Plants require a shady location and grow best in organically-rich loamy soils. In suitable situations they can be quite fast growing. Plants must not be allowed to dry out and if necessary should be watered during dry spells. Mulches are beneficial. Seed germinates readily within two months of sowing.

The fronds and fruit of *Pinanga kuhlii*.

TRIANGLE PALM

Neodypsis decaryi

The genus *Neodypsis* contains about fourteen species of palms all endemic to the island of Madagascar. Little appears to have been written about palms of this genus and it would seem that they are in need of study by a specialist. All species have a solitary trunk and feathery fronds.

The Triangle Palm is quite remarkable and is the only member of the genus to be grown to any extent. Its unusual common name arises because its fronds are arranged in three vertical rows creating a three-sided trunk. A second unusual feature is found in the lower-most leaflets of the fronds. These leaflets have long filamentous extensions which hang to the ground like reins. In the unexpanded leaves these tie the leaflets together.

Neodypsis decaryi grows to about 6 m in height. Its frond bases are covered with chalky white powder and wool. The fronds are held stiffly erect and the leaflets are grey. All in all it is a very distinctive palm which should become popular in cultivation. Plants appear to be fairly easy to grow and will succeed in tropical and subtropical regions. They require a sunny position in well drained soil.

Neodypsis decaryi.

PADDLE LEAF PALM

Phoenicophorium borsigianum

The exotic appearance of this palm is the epitome of the tropics. The large fronds are undivided (except when split by wind) and may grow to 2 m long and 1 m broad. They are deep green and have prominent ribs where the main veins run. The leaf margins are regularly incised to impart an attractive symmetric appearance.

Juvenile plants of this palm develop an upright crown of fronds, whereas in older plants which have developed a trunk, many of the fronds arch downwards. The trunk itself is slender (spiny when young) and may grow to more than 12 m tall. Hanging clusters (about 1 m long) of small yellowish-red fruit are an added decorative feature.

Paddle Leaf Palm is native to the Seychelles islands and is reportedly still common in its native state. Being very sensitive to cold, plants require tropical conditions. They prefer an open aspect exposed to some sun but protected from severe winds which damage their large fronds. They are an excellent potted subject for a heated glasshouse or conservatory.

This palm was previously known as *Stevensonia borsigiana*.

Phoenicophorium borsigianum. Photo Dennis Hundscheidt

CANARY ISLAND DATE PALM

Phoenix canariensis

This palm's natural distribution is restricted to the tiny pieces of land that comprise the Canary Islands. Despite this it is a very familiar palm because of its popularity in many countries around the world. Plants thrive in cultivation and can be successfully grown in a wide range of climates from tropical to temperate and from coastal to inland districts. Although it will succeed in the tropics plants grow better in milder climates and they are very tolerant of heavy frosts.

In Australia it is a familiar sight and appears to have been a much more popular subject for cultivation earlier this century than it is nowadays. It is very noticeable in municipal parks and larger private gardens where plants have sufficient room to spread. It is probably the most familiar palm grown in inland towns and is also often seen around homesteads on farms. Plants obviously thrive in the climate experienced in these inland districts for their leaves have a healthy lustre and the clusters of flowers and fruit are intensely coloured.

Canary Island Date Palm will succeed in quite poor soils, including those of low fertility. It does not succeed where the drainage is poor and other palms should be used if these conditions prevail. A sunny position is essential. Plants respond to the application of mulches and fertilisers. They are very hardy to dryness but appreciate watering during long periods of dry weather. It should be noted that the basal leaflets of this palm (as with all species of *Phoenix*) are very spiny and can inflict a painful wound. Fallen fronds and those removed by pruning should be handled with care.

Phoenix canariensis is a large palm and must be given sufficient room to spread. It develops a thick woody trunk to 20 m tall (usually less in cultivation) and this is covered with knobbly scars left by fallen fronds. The crown is impressively large and dense consisting of up to one hundred fronds. Each frond is about 6 m long and is dark green with numerous closely spaced slender leaflets. Flower clusters are produced in profusion among the leaves and form conspicuous blotches of yellow. Each plant is of a single sex and on the female plants the large clusters of orange fruit make a colourful display. The fruit have a layer of edible flesh but are not particularly palatable. Seeds germinate readily within two to four months of sowing.

Phoenix canariensis.

DATE PALM

Phoenix dactylifera

Dates are a very ancient crop which has been improved by human selection over thousands of years. They are so ancient that today the species is virtually unknown in the wild, although it is believed to have originated in northern Africa. Dates, as a crop, have been cultivated for over 5000 years and the fruit is an important part of the diet of millions of people. Date flesh is very low in protein and fats but is energy rich with some cultivars having up to 60 per cent of sugar.

Date plants are either male or female and are commonly propagated from suckers. Plants are very long living and may fruit for more than 100 years, each year yielding about 50 kg of fruit (3000-5000 individual fruit).

Plants are very easily grown and will tolerate almost any climate (they are grown from temperate to tropical regions, in coastal, inland and mountainous districts). For successful fruit production however they need sunny, warm, dry climates with low rainfall and low humidity. Access to ground water will ensure strong growth.

The Date Palm, *Phoenix dactylifera*.

CLIFF DATE PALM

Phoenix rupicola

A native to India, this palm obtains the common name from its habit of growing among rocks on the sides of cliffs and gorges in the Himalayas and other mountains of northern India. It is a beautiful palm which has become well entrenched in cultivation, but still deserves to be much more widely planted.

Plants of the Cliff Date Palm have a single fairly slender woody trunk scarred by the remains of fallen leaves, and a graceful crown of light to dark green feathery fronds. These fronds arch and twist in the crown and the older fronds are nearly pendulous. Each plant is unisexual and male and female plants are necessary for fruit production. The branched inflorescences arise among the leaves and bear masses of small cream to pale yellow flowers. The oblong, shiny purple-brown fruit are about 2 cm long and have a thin layer of edible flesh.

Phoenix rupicola is a very easy palm to grow and is attractive from an early age. It will grow in a variety of positions, including shade, but must have good drainage. Once established plants are quite hardy to dryness, but for best growth and appearance should be watered regularly.

Phoenix rupicola.

SENEGAL DATE PALM

Phoenix reclinata

A versatile palm for horticulture, this species can be successfully cultivated in regions ranging from tropical to temperate and in coastal as well as inland districts. It was a popular species in the latter half of the last century and the many large specimens which now grace our parks and public gardens are the result of that popularity. In fact it is one of the best clumping palms available for parks and gardens provided it is given room to spread. Clumps are excellent as specimens in lawns, as a border for paths or as a backdrop for ponds, lakes or other water features.

Senegal Date Palm is also known as African Date Palm, Wild Date Palm, Coffee Palm and Feather Palm. It is native to the continent of Africa where it is widespread from tropical to temperate regions, usually growing in damp soils. Plants are variable and may be stemless, shortly stemmed or with tall prominent trunks.

In its native state this palm has many uses. The heart (cabbage) is eaten and the flower stalks are cut off and the collected sap is con-verted to an alcoholic drink. The fruit is edible but not particularly tasty. The midribs of the leaves are plaited to make mats and fibres from the leaf sheaths are made into brushes and brooms.

Senegal Date Palm is a graceful species with slender woody grey trunks that may be straight or curved. Each trunk has a crown of arching bright green feathery fronds. Adjacent crowns intermingle to present a dense appear-ance. Each plant is either a male or female. The small cream flowers are borne in dense clusters among the leaves and on female plants these are followed by yellowish date-like fruit about 2 cm long.

The basal leaflets on each frond of this palm have a dagger-like point which can inflict a painful wound. This is the only drawback to its cultivation and plants should not be sited too close to pathways.

An open sunny position is necessary for this species and the soil should drain freely. Even poorly fertile or shallow soils can be suc-cessful. Plants like plenty of water and respond to the application of fertilisers. Propagation from fresh seed is easy and suckers can also be successfully removed.

A clump of *Phoenix reclinata*.

DWARF DATE PALM

Phoenix roebelenii

This is undoubtedly the most popular species of *Phoenix* in cultivation. Plants achieve manageable dimensions and have a neat attractive appearance which appeals to growers. Their root system is not excessive and can be confined to a tub or some other container for many years without setback. Plants can even be successfully used for indoor decoration, however they require a brightly lit position.

Although common in cultivation, the origin of this palm was obscure for many years until it was established recently that it is native to Laos (along the Mekong River). Although this is a very tropical habitat the species is, in fact, adaptable to other climates and can even be successfully grown as far south as Melbourne. Plants, however, thrive best in subtropical and tropical climates and they are a very familiar sight in parks, gardens and are even planted in tubs, etc. around shopping centres. They look particularly appealing when associated with water features.

The Dwarf Date Palm rarely grows more than 2.5 m to 3 m tall. Plants have a slender woody trunk that is covered with prominent hard projections. The fronds arch gracefully in a rounded crown and the lower ones may be almost pendulous. Each frond is about 1.5 m long and is an attractive bright green. Short dense clusters of cream flowers arise among the fronds and are followed by small black fruit. Each plant is either male or female and group planting is necessary for viable seeds to be formed. The fruit have a thin layer of edible flesh surrounding the seed.

For cultivation a sunny situation is necessary, although this palm has proved to be very adaptable and will grow in partial shade or filtered sun. Plants are often grown singly, however this is an excellent palm for group planting. Soils must drain freely as this species can be susceptible to waterlogging of the roots. Given good drainage this palm will grow happily in a wide range of soil types, including those which are poorly fertile. Once established, plants are very tolerant of dryness and watering is rarely necessary except perhaps in long dry periods. Application of fertilisers and mulching of the soil surface are beneficial practices.

A grouped planting of the Dwarf Date Palm,
Phoenix roebelenii.

SILVER DATE PALM

Phoenix sylvestris

In India, where it is native, this is a common palm which is of significance to the local people. The sap which exudes when the flower stalks are cut off, is used extensively for making sugar (the sap is boiled until the sugar crystallises). Wild stands are tapped and the species is also extensively planted in groves specifically for sugar production. The leaves also are useful and are woven into bags or baskets, or used for brooms. Fibre for rope-making can be obtained from the leaf stems. The fruit is edible but not particularly palatable.

Silver Date Palm is a handsome ornamental. It is faster growing than most other species of *Phoenix* and develops a characteristically rounded crown of grey-green to bluish fronds. This crown tops a slender woody trunk which is patterned roughly by the bases of fallen leaves.

Silver Date Palm is very adaptable. Soils can be quite poor or rich and be poorly or well drained. Tropical and temperate climates can be equally suitable, although plants are slower growing in the latter. It is also suited to inland regions. Two plants are necessary for seed production.

Phoenix sylvestris.

HAWAIIAN FAN PALM

Pritchardia guadichaudii

The genus *Pritchardia* consists of some thirty-six species of decorative palms scattered on the Pacific islands of Hawaii and Fiji. They are renowned for their heavy crown of large, stiff pleated leaves. They are majestic palms which epitomise the tropics. A couple of species have become widely planted in tropical countries.

Pritchardia guadichaudii is native to the Hawaiian island of Molokai. It grows on vertical cliffs near the sea and in suitable situations occurs in colonies. The soil is of volcanic origin and the rainfall is high.

Pritchardia guadichaudii is a very handsome subject for cultivation. It is one of a few members of the genus which will tolerate some cold and plants grow very well in subtropical regions, as well as further north. There are many attractive specimens around Brisbane. A sunny aspect is necessary for its cultivation.

Plants of this species develop a relatively slender trunk topped with a crown of heavily pleated leaves which may be more than 1 m across. Mature leaves are bright green. Young leaves are covered with white wool which is shed as they expand.

Propagation is from seed which takes two to four months to germinate.

Pritchardia guadichaudii.

WINDOW PANE PALM

Reinhardtia gracilis

Reinhardtia is a small genus of five species of palm distributed in Mexico, Central and South America. They were formerly well known in the genus *Malortiea*. They are delicate clumping palms with thin, prominently ringed stems (usually green) and short leaves which are either arranged in a crown or scattered along the stems. The leaves may be entire and undivided or are divided into a few broad segments which are unevenly toothed on the apex. All species of *Reinhardtia* are small palms which grow in rainforests and jungles. They are mostly found in the lowlands of tropical regions but may also extend to over 1000 m altitude.

Only one species of *Reinhardtia* is grown to any extent in Australia. Other species are well worthy of introduction because they have a graceful habit, interesting foliage and are of very manageable dimensions. All species need shade and must never be allowed to dry out. Soils must be well drained and preferably have a high humus content.

The Window Pane Palm is so called because there are small gaps or 'windows' between the main veins at the base of each leaflet. These 'windows' create interest in the palm and it has become well known and sought after by collectors as well as the general public. It makes an excellent container plant as its root system does not mind being confined. Because it is slow growing, plants may need repotting only every two to three years. An open fibrous mix, well fortified with organic material, is suitable for its culture. It has proved to be a useful palm for indoor decoration and will tolerate fairly low light levels, although plants do not like a dry atmosphere.

Window Pane Palm can be grown outdoors in tropical and subtropical regions. Plants are tolerant of some cold during winter but are very sensitive to drying of the root system (they rarely recover from such an occurrence). It also needs protection from direct sun, as the leaves bleach and burn badly if they are exposed to any extent. Mulching of the soil surface and watering during dry periods are important for good growth and development.

Plants of the Window Pane Palm rarely grow more than 1.5 m tall and the stems are only about 1 cm thick. Propagation can be by careful division of the clumps or from seed which germinates readily within two months of sowing.

The Window Pane Palm, *Reinhardtia gracilis*.

LADY PALM

Rhapis excelsa

Although this species is widely cultivated in many parts of the world, there are no authenticated records of plants occurring naturally in the wild. While its origin is believed to be somewhere in southern China, this is in need of confirmation.

The Lady Palm forms dense multi-stemmed clumps that are leafy to ground level, therefore it is one of the few small palms that makes an effective screen or windbreak. The closely placed stems are very slender and are covered with interlaced brown fibres. The leaves are scattered up the stems (which grow to 2.5 m tall) and have six to eleven widely diverging segments that are stiff and spreading or held partly erect and with no tendency to droop. The leaves are light green and generally take on a yellowish hue if the plants are starved or grown in full sun. Short, stiff branched inflorescences arise in the upper leaf bases and are covered with creamy-yellow flowers. Plants are either male or female and both sexes must be in close proximity for viable seed production. The fruit is small, round, white and fleshy.

Lady Palm is one of the best garden palms with its popularity being limited only by its availability and price (large plants are very expensive). Plants will grow in climates ranging from tropical to temperate. They will tolerate considerable exposure to sun if well watered on a regular basis, however the leaves will bleach badly and burn if watering is neglected. For best appearance this palm should be grown in a semi-protected position where it only receives partial sunlight during the day. It can be established under large trees and will make satisfactory growth providing it is mulched and kept moist. As a tub plant it is unsurpassed and will remain in the same container for years without the need for repotting. Indoors the plants are very decorative and will last for long periods before a spell outdoors becomes necessary.

Most propagation of this palm is by division of the clumps. Plants can be divided readily (especially in spring when new growth is underway), however the divisions may take considerable time to establish. Aerial layers can also be successfully used.

In Japan a number of choice cultivars of Lady Palm are regarded as valuable collectors' items. These are mainly variations which have variegated leaf segments. Some of these have been imported into Australia but at this stage they are still rare. Two such cultivars having variegated leaves are illustrated in the accompanying plates.

A cultivar of Rhapis excelsa with variegated leaves.

A cultivar of Rhapis excelsa with young leaves pale yellow-green.

DWARF LADY PALM

Rhapis sp.

The genus *Rhapis* consists of twelve species of palms occurring in southern China, South-East Asia and extending to Indonesia. All are highly ornamental small palms and a few species have become firm favourites in cultivation. They are valued for their clumping habit and appealing leaves which are deeply divided into narrow segments which spread like the fingers of a hand. The clumps are generally very dense and increase by the production of new suckers at the margins. The stems are very slender and are covered throughout by closely woven brown fibres. Leaves are scattered along the stems and are not borne in a crown.

In their natural state *Rhapis* palms grow in tropical and subtropical rainforests and jungles. Two or three species have become popular horticultural subjects in Australia and are in constant demand by enthusiasts and gardeners alike. Large specimens command high prices.

Rhapis palms were very popular last century and early this century and were widely planted in private gardens, as well as parks, municipal and botanical gardens. They were commonly planted as a border to paths or as a backdrop to water features. Large clumps are still a prominent feature of many public parks and gardens. Although these palms are of tropical origin, the cultivated species grow extremely well in temperate climates. They are also particularly suited for use as potted specimens indoors and will withstand both neglect and fairly dark conditions. Plants will grow happily in containers for a few years without the need for repotting. An open fibrous mix, well fortified with organic material, is suitable for repotting.

In the garden, plants are best situated where they will be protected from extremes of sun and wind. Excessive sun bleaches the leaves and results in dead tips on the frond segments. Plants will survive in such conditions (especially if well watered) but look untidy. Mulches and fertilisers are beneficial.

The Dwarf Lady Palm is believed to originate in Japan. It is often sold in nurseries as *Rhapis excelsa* 'Dwarf' but appears to be distinct from that species. It can be distinguished by the fewer leaf segments (three to six) which are widely spaced, and often elliptical in shape, and the very sparse inflorescence. It is an excellent palm for tub culture and indoor decoration. Seed germinates readily.

The Dwarf Lady Palm, *Rhapis sp.*

NIKAU PALM

Rhopalostylis sapida

Nikau Palm is a native of New Zealand where it is very widespread over the North Island and much of the South Island. It grows in dense lowland forests seeming to prefer moist, protected situations. Visitors to New Zealand commonly notice this palm in paddocks where it has been retained during clearing operations. Its distinctive silhouette of upright fronds and a bulging crownshaft is reminiscent of a feather-duster or shuttlecock.

Nikau Palm was of importance to the New Zealand Maoris who ate both the young inflorescence and the heart of the crown. The leaves were plaited into baskets and other utensils and were also used to thatch hut roofs. The fruit of this palm is so hard that it is said to have been used as bullets when shot was scarce.

Nikau Palm is best suited to temperate regions. Plants are very slow growing and do not begin to form a trunk until they are about 15 years of age. They need a sheltered position, well drained soil and plenty of moisture. Propagation is from seed which takes three to four months to germinate.

The Nikau Palm, *Rhopalostylis sapida*.

CUBAN ROYAL PALM

Roystonea regia

The genus *Roystonea* contains six species of very distinctive palms. They are distributed from Florida to South America and the West Indies. All species have a solitary fairly stout grey trunk (variously thickened) with a prominent green crown shaft and a spreading crown of feathery fronds. They grow in colonies in low-lying areas which may be subject to periodic inundation.

Cuban Royal Palm is one of the most popular species in cultivation. It originates from Cuba but the species is widely planted in many countries around the world. Tropical and sub-tropical climates are particularly suitable but plants can also be successful in warm temperate climates. It is an excellent palm for planting in avenues and is often used for this purpose in municipal gardens.

Cuban Royal Palms can be quite fast growing, especially if liberally supplied with water, organic mulches and fertilisers rich in nitrogen. Plants thrive in wet soils. They need a sunny situation.

This palm can be distinguished from other species of *Roystonea* by its bulging trunk (near the centre) and the arrangement of its leaflets. It is a stately palm and an excellent choice as a specimen plant.

The Cuban Royal Palm, *Roystonea regia*.

PUERTO RICAN HAT PALM

Sabal causiarum

The leaves of some fan palms can be used
to produce light fibre hats that provide excellent
protection from the heat of the sun. This is true of
the Puerto Rican Hat Palm from Puerto Rico. Its
leaves are collected when fairly young and
soaked in boiling water to separate the fibrous
segments. These are dried and can then be
plaited into hats.

Sabal causiarum is a difficult palm to mis-
identify. Its stocky grey trunk may be about 1 m
across and 10 m tall and yet is of even width
throughout. Its crown always appears as if
abbreviated and the lower dead fronds hang for
some time before shedding. They are deeply
divided into segments and when fresh are often
bluish-green. The inflorescences, which are
about as long as the leaves (or longer), bear
masses of small white flowers. These are
followed by round black fruit about
1 cm across.

Puerto Rican Hat Palm is somewhat ungainly
in appearance, but is nevertheless an interesting
and distinctive species. It will grow well in
tropical and temperate regions and also thrives
in the drier atmosphere of inland districts. It is an
excellent palm to line a driveway or for avenue
planting. Propagation is from seed which takes
about two months to germinate. Seedlings
are generally slow growing.

The Puerto Rican Hat Palm, *Sabal causiarum*.

DWARF PALMETTO PALM

Sabal minor

This dwarf palm is somewhat variable, lacking a trunk in some forms while others develop a woody trunk 1 – 2 m tall. Even those plants which are apparently trunkless have some sort of woody subterranean structure. The large fan-shaped leaves, to 2 m long, spread in a stiff crown. They are often bluish-green and are deeply divided into stiff segments. Slender inflorescences may be 3 m or 4 m long and bear thousands of small white flowers which are strongly fragrant. These are followed by globular shiny black fruit about 1 cm across. Often a series of inflorescences may be produced during the summer.

Sabal minor is a very hardy palm which could be more widely planted since its dimensions are never excessive. It, however, lacks any distinctive feature and is generally by-passed when a choice is made.

Plants require good drainage but are not fussy as to soil type and will grow successfully on quite shallow soils. They must have a situation exposed to some sun and good air movement as excess shade will cause rapid plant death. Dwarf Palmetto is native to some southern States of the USA. It can be readily propagated from seed.

The Dwarf Palmetto Palm, *Sabal minor*.

PALMETTO PALM

Sabal palmetto

Sabal palms are amongst the hardiest of all palms. The genus consists of about fourteen species found in the USA, Mexico, Central America and the West Indies. They are sun-loving hardy palms which lack prickles. The leaves are fan-shaped and have a midrib which may be short or runs through the leaf depending on the species. The leaves may have a characteristic twist. In some species the trunk is subterranean while others have a woody erect trunk which varies from slender to quite stout.

Sabal palms tend to have a characteristic silhouette and by nature are sturdy or stocky plants. They are notoriously difficult to identify, particularly those of cultivated origin. Hybridism is common and a number of the characteristics used to separate species are not constant.

Sabal palmetto is one of the easier species to identify. Plants develop a sturdy grey trunk which is covered (at least in the upper part) by an interlaced network of pale-coloured leaf bases. The crown is dense and rounded. The leaves are blue-green with a characteristic twist and tend to arch downwards at the end. A strong rib runs the full length of the leaf blade. Large clusters of white flowers arise among the leaves and are followed by small, black round fruit which are borne in profusion.

Palmetto Palm is native to south-eastern USA particularly Florida. It grows in colonies in low-lying areas, often in coastal districts. It is sometimes called the Cabbage Palmetto because of its tasty heart which was widely eaten by Indians in the area where it grows. They also ate the fruit, which though small, is produced in large quantities. The sap collected by cutting off a developing inflorescence can be used to make wine.

Palmetto Palm is fairly popular in cultivation. It grows well in areas with a mild climate, particularly warm temperate and subtropical regions. Plants are often seen in parks and to a lesser extent home gardens. It is generally planted singly but also lends itself well to group planting (see colour plate). Best growth is in sandy soil, where its roots have access to ground water. In such situations plants can be fairly fast growing. It is a useful palm for coastal districts and will tolerate some exposure to salt-laden winds. Plants may flower and fruit when quite young. Seed germinates readily but it may take six months or longer before the seedlings appear.

A grouped planting of *Sabal palmetto*.

SAW PALMETTO PALM

Serenoa repens

The Saw Palmetto is endemic to the USA where it is restricted to the south-eastern States of South Carolina, Georgia, Florida, Alabama and Mississippi. It is most common on the coastal plain and may form extensive colonies (in some areas it forms thickets so dense as to be impenetrable). Only a single species is known in the genus *Serenoa*.

The Saw Palmetto is a fan palm with a trunk that is usually subterranean but sometimes emergent and reaching 3 m tall. The trunks branch freely to form a clump. Each trunk is fairly slender and is covered with shaggy hair arising on the persistent leaf bases. The fronds are held stiffly erect and arise on slender stalks which have noticeable prickly teeth. The blades are deeply divided into many slender stiff segments and are bluish-green in colour. In some forms they may be yellowish or a splendid silvery-white. Branched inflorescences about 1 m long arise among the leaves and carry white flowers. Ripe fruit are purple-black and have an unusual smell. These fruit have a layer of edible flesh and were eaten by local Indian tribes of the area.

Saw Palmettos are an attractive palm for cultivation. They are rather cold sensitive however and only grow best in tropical or warm subtropical regions. An excellent palm for coastal districts they will tolerate considerable exposure to salt-laden winds. Plants grow very well in sandy soils, particularly if their roots have access to ground water. They need a sunny aspect and will withstand full sunshine even when quite small. Once established, plants are very hardy to dryness. Mulching of the soil surface and application of complete fertiliser is beneficial to growth.

Saw Palmettos are easily propagated from seed which takes three to six months to germinate. Seedlings are generally slow growing and may not be ready to plant out for a few years after germination.

The Saw Palmetto, *Serenoa repens*. Photo Bruce Gray

BRITTLE THATCH PALM

Thrinax morrisii

The genus *Thrinax* consists of four species of palms which occur naturally in the Caribbean region between Florida and the West Indies. All are commonly known as Thatch Palms because the stiff fronds are used for thatching local dwellings.

Thrinax morrisii is a very slender species with a woody grey trunk to 10 m tall and a somewhat untidy crown of fan-shaped leaves. Each leaf is about 3 m long and consists of a very slender stalk and a bright green blade which is divided about half way into stiff segments. Slender inflorescences (much longer than the leaves) arise among the leaf bases and bear small white flowers. These are followed by prominent bunches of round white fruit each about 6 cm across.

Brittle Thatch Palm is an attractive species and its very slender habit means that plants are readily accommodated in small gardens. It is most suitable for tropical and subtropical regions and plants grow especially well in coastal districts. Unfortunately they are slow growing. They will take sun from an early age and do not mind calcareous soils. Seeds germinate within about four months of sowing.

The Brittle Thatch Palm, *Thrinax morrisii*.

88

CHINESE WINDMILL PALM or CHUSAN PALM

Trachycarpus fortunei

This is one of the hardiest palms for a cold climate. Plants will withstand heavy frosts and even periods when they are covered by snow. The species is well adapted to these conditions as frosts and snow are common in the mountainous regions of China where it occurs naturally.

Chinese Windmill Palm is also adaptable and can be successfully grown in warm temperate and subtropical climates. It does not thrive in the tropics however. As well as being common in private gardens, plants are a familiar sight in public parks and municipal gardens, usually growing singly.

Chinese Windmill Palm is a slow but steady grower in temperate regions, but is faster in the subtropics. Plants have a slender woody trunk that is covered with a coarse, matted brown fibre (which is excellent for lining hanging baskets) and a compact crown of stiff fan-shaped fronds. These are dark green (greyish beneath) and are deeply divided into slender segments. The flower clusters are showy, being a bright yellow blotch in the dark crown. The kidney-shaped fruit are pale blue. This palm is still occasionally sold in nurseries (wrongly) as Chamaerops excelsa.

The Chinese Windmill Palm, Trachycarpus fortunei, in flower. Photo Chris Goudey

DWARF FISHTAIL PALM

Wallichia densiflora

The common name of Fishtail Palm normally applies to species of *Caryota*, but this dwarf palm has leaflets of a similar shape to that group. It is a suckering species which forms very dense clumps that may grow to 3 m across. Individual fronds may be 2 m long and are divided into large leaflets. These are roughly fishtail-shaped and have wavy, toothed or lobed margins. The upper side is bright shiny green while the underneath is silvery-white. The fronds move readily in any breeze and the contrast between the upper and lower surfaces is then quite apparent.

The trunks of this palm are virtually subterranean and each bears a cluster of fronds at its apex. The inflorescences are generally shorter than the leaves and the small bisexual flowers are followed by dense clusters of purplish-black fruit. Each fruit is about 1.5 cm long and softens when ripe.

Dwarf Fishtail Palm deserves to become more widely planted. Its clumps are neat and bushy and the fronds have a decorative appearance. Plants are slow growing (especially when young), but should be given sufficient room to spread. They like a situation protected from excessive sun and wind. Although established plants are quite hardy to dryness, for best appearance they should be watered regularly. Mulches and light dressings with nitrogenous fertiliser are generally beneficial. Plants are able to withstand light to moderate frosts without excessive damage.

Native to shady moist gullies of the Himalayas in northern India, this palm can be grown in subtropical and temperate regions. It is an excellent border for paths and garden beds. Propagation is from seed or by division of the clumps. Seed is generally slow and erratic to germinate.

The genus *Wallichia* contains six species including the remarkable *Wallichia disticha*, which has its fronds arranged in two vertical rows on opposite sides of the trunk, imparting a flat profile to the plants. All species of *Wallichia* occur naturally in the Himalayan region of northern India, Bangladesh and southern China.

A clump of *Wallichia densiflora*.

AMERICAN COTTON PALM

Washingtonia filifera

From an early age, plants of this species have a much sturdier habit than the slender, but very similar, *Washingtonia robusta*. Mature specimens can be identified by their stout tapering trunk. Other than the relative thickness of the trunk both species are remarkably similar. Occasionally mature specimens are seen which have a 'petticoat' of overlapping persistent dead fronds almost to ground level. This can be a feature of both species of *Washingtonia* but all too often the hanging fronds are vandalised by fire and irreplaceably destroyed.

American Cotton Palm is native to the American states of California and Arizona as well as Mexico. It grows in canyons around permanent water and forms impressive colonies. The species adapts extremely well to cultivation and is widely planted in temperate Australia, succeeding especially well in inland towns. It is a useful palm for planting in avenues, as a specimen in lawns or in groups if given sufficient space to spread. Plants are very easy to grow requiring sunshine, good drainage and access to water.

The name Cotton Palm arises from numerous white threads on the leaves which are white and cottony. This feature is most obvious on young plants. Propagation is from seed with the seed germinating within two months.

Washingtonia filifera has a fat trunk.

WASHINGTON PALM or SKYDUSTER

Washingtonia robusta

The genus Washingtonia consists of two species
of palm, both very similar in general appearance.
Both species are commonly planted in temperate and subtropical regions of Australia and large
old specimens are a relatively common sight.

Washingtonia robusta has a much more slender
trunk that Washingtonia filifera and may also grow
taller. The base of the grey, woody trunk is
swollen and then tapers upwards to the rounded
crown of shiny, fan-shaped fronds. Long slender
inflorescences which bear small pink to cream
bisexual flowers hang from among the fronds.
This is an excellent way to distinguish these
palms from species of Livistona which bear their
flower clusters well within the fronds. Large
numbers of round brown fruit (about the size of a
pea) are borne on each inflorescence.

Washingtonia robusta is native to north-
western Mexico where it grows in rocky gorges
and gullies around permanent water. It is a
distinctive palm worth growing for its silhouette.
The species lends itself well to group planting. It
is easily grown in a wide variety of soils and once
established is quite hardy to dryness and neglect. Seeds germinate easily but the seedlings
are relatively slow growing.

A grouped planting of Washingtonia robusta. This
palm has a very slender trunk.

INDEX